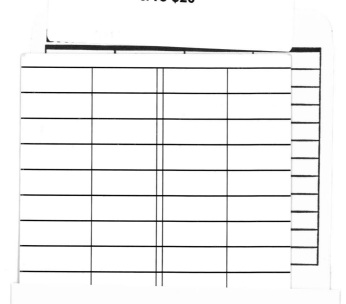

Children of the World

My Life in
BRAZIL

Patience Coster

Cavendish Square

New York

Published in 2015 by Cavendish Square Publishing, LLC
243 5th Avenue, Suite 136, New York, NY 10016

Website: cavendishsq.com

This publication represents the opinions and views of the author based on his or her personal experience, knowledge, and research. The information in this book serves as a general guide only. The author and publisher have used their best efforts in preparing this book and disclaim liability rising directly or indirectly from the use and application of this book.

CPSIA Compliance Information: Batch #WW15CSQ

All websites were available and accurate when this book was sent to press.

Library of Congress Cataloging-in-Publication Data

Coster, Patience.
My life in Brazil / by Patience Coster.
p. cm. — (Children of the world)
Includes index.
ISBN 978-1-50260-044-8 (hardcover) ISBN 978-1-50260-041-7 (paperback) ISBN 978-1-50260-039-4 (ebook)
1. Brazil — Juvenile literature. 2. Children — Brazil — Juvenile literature. 3. Brazil — Social life and customs — Juvenile literature. I. Coster, Patience. II. Title.
F2508.5 C695 2015
981—d23

Printed in the United States of America

Contents

Waking Up

Olá! My name is Valentina. I am ten years old. I live in Bela Vista, a **rural community** near the city of Araraquara in Brazil.

Here I am, dreaming of the moon and stars. I want to be an **astronomer** when I grow up.

I share a house with my parents and my brother, Rafael, who is thirteen years older than I am.

Valentina says... I get up at the same time every day. The sun wakes me – I don't need an alarm!

My Country

I live in Brazil, the largest country in South America. It has a **4,655-mile (7,491-km)** coastline along the Atlantic Ocean. One third of all the people in South America live in Brazil!

Getting Dressed

I get ready for school. We don't have a uniform, so I can wear what I like. It's cold first thing, so I'll need to take my sweater.

I brush my hair – I have to tie it back for school.

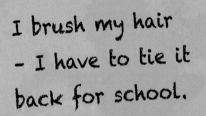

It's February, the start of the school year and early summer in Brazil.

Valentina says ...
I wash my face and brush my teeth. I'm ready to go now!

Climate and Weather

In Bela Vista, the climate is warm all year round. It rains a lot in summer, but is quite dry in winter.

Walking to School

The school is close to my house – it doesn't take long to get there. It's nice walking when it's sunny.

My cousin Luiz attends the same school, so he walks with me.

There are lots of students in Brazil, and not everyone goes to school at the same time. We go to the first session. There are two other sessions later in the day.

8

We join the line for breakfast. All the students sit down to eat together.

Valentina says ...
We have bread and butter and hot chocolate for breakfast.

The School Year

There are two school terms each year. The first is from February to June and the second is from August to December.

Lessons Begin

The students get together for assembly. The head teacher reads out a quote or short story with an important message.

We sing the anthem of Brazil. Students hold up the national flag.

After this, our lessons begin. I am in fifth grade. This morning we have classes in math, geography, science, and Portuguese language.

Valentina says ...

I've made a **relief map** showing the rivers and mountains of our country.

I help the teacher find Bela Vista on the map.

The Amazon

The world's second-longest river, the Amazon, flows through Brazil. It is surrounded by the Amazon rainforest, the biggest rainforest on the planet.

Break Time

10.00 AM

We've been working hard, so we're happy to go out to play for a while.

Before eating, we have to wash our hands to get rid of any germs.

Valentina says ...

We have fruit at break time. I eat outside with my friends.

Many fruits grow in Brazil – oranges, mangoes, pineapples, bananas, and some you might not have heard of like **açai** *(ah-sah-EE)*, **carambola** and **pinha**.

When we have finished eating, we play hopscotch.

I throw a stone into the shapes on the ground. Then I jump through the spaces to pick up the stone.

Fun and Games

As well as hopscotch, we play games like What's the Time, Mr. Wolf? and marbles. For birthday parties, we play at smashing the **piñata**.

13

Back to Work!

In science, we learn about different types of food and where they come from. We cut out pictures and make a collage.

Valentina says...
I cut out pictures of foods of animal origin for a classroom display.

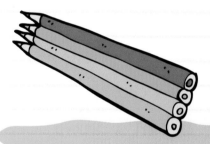

Our school gives us books, pencils, scissors, and rulers, but sometimes there aren't enough to go around.

In Portuguese language class we have a test. Then we grade one another's work.

We do homework in the last session before lunch.

Speaking Portuguese

In Brazil, the main language is Portuguese. We say "*Bom dia*" (BOAM-dee-uh) for "Good morning" and "*Boa noite*"(BOW-noit) for "Good night".

Lunchtime

I eat lunch in school every day. The meals are great! Most of the ingredients come from local suppliers.

Valentina says...

It's sausage, beans, and rice for lunch today – yum!

We have very healthy meals – there are always fruits, vegetables, and **pulses** offered.

The cost of our meals is **subsidized** (partly paid) by the government.

When lunch is finished we brush our teeth and get ready for the afternoon's classes.

Brazilian Food

Bean stew with pork and rice is popular in Brazil. *Pão de queijo* (POW-oh dey Kwee-I-joe) – a type of cheese bun made with **cassava** or corn flour – is delicious eaten hot from the oven.

More Lessons

It's time for computer class. Afterwards we watch a video about the culture of Brazil.

Valentina says ...

We practice our typing using a text about the traditions of Easter.

Easter is an important festival in Brazil. People carry religious statues in parades through the streets.

18

In cultural studies we watch a video on Brazilian **folklore**.

Today we find out about Curupira, a red-haired boy with backwards facing feet who lives in the forest and protects it from harm.

Religion in Brazil

Most people in Brazil are Roman Catholics, but more and more are becoming Protestants. Belief in the power of the spirit world is also widespread.

School's Out

School's finished, so I meet up with Luiz and we walk home. We have lots of time left to play!

Valentina says ...

What shall we do this afternoon, Luiz?

I love the way the houses in this street are painted different rainbow colors.

I get home, have a snack and a drink, and change my clothes. Luiz and I meet up again with our bikes.

It's great to ride our bikes in the fresh air and sunshine.

Town and Country

Our nearest city, Araraquara, is 172 miles (278 km) from São Paulo, the largest city in South America. São Paulo is a huge business center full of steel, concrete, and glass skyscrapers.

Helping at Home

There is a market garden not far from our house. My mom has asked me to go and buy some vegetables.

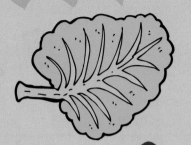

I pay the man 2 R$ (Brazilian reals) for three lettuces. It is a good price.

I help my mom with the housework. We are lucky because the tap water in our house is safe to drink. Some families don't have a clean water supply.

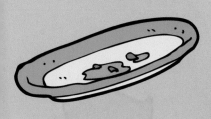

Valentina says...

I'm washing the dishes in an old shirt. I don't want to ruin my new one!

School and Family

In Brazil, children start school at age five and are expected to stay until they are fifteen. But some drop out early because they need to find paid work to support their families.

Downtime

Luiz has a pet parakeet which he keeps in his room. She is very friendly. I go to Luiz' house to play with her.

Valentina says ...

I love it when the parakeet kisses me!

There are many beautiful birds in Brazil, from hummingbirds and parrots to **spoonbills** and birds of prey like the **caracara**.

We live near a field of wild flowers. I feel proud to live in a country with such wonderful, colorful wildlife.

The flowers are so tall I can hardly see the other side of the field!

Animal Heaven

Brazil has the greatest variety of animals of any country in the world. There are 600 mammal species and 1,600 bird species living here.

Hobbies

My favorite hobby is reading comics. I like "Monica's Gang" by cartoonist Maurício de Sousa.

Valentina says...

It's great that Monica always beats the bullies!

Comics are very popular in Brazil. I've collected over eighty comic books and read them all many times.

I do some schoolwork or surf the Internet, watching films and reading stories.

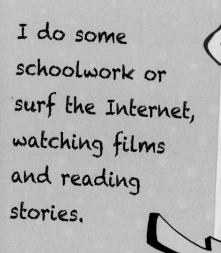

If it's really hot I go out for ice cream. I love sweets like coconut and peanut candy, but I'm not allowed to eat them until after my dinner.

Popular Culture

Brazil has one of the largest TV networks in the world. The most popular programs are soap operas. Any channel showing soccer, which we call football, will also have a huge audience.

Dinner and Bedtime

Now it's time for dinner with my family. We enjoy talking and eating in front of the television.

My dad and brother like the news programs. My mom and I like the soaps.

I can see millions of stars above my house. When I'm a famous astronomer I will know all their names!

The Night Sky

The skies are so dark in Bela Vista that we can see the Milky Way. The most famous **constellation** of the **Southern Hemisphere**, the Southern Cross, is featured on the Brazilian national flag.

Glossary

açai A purple berry from a South American palm tree.

astronomer A person whose job it is to study the sun, moon, stars, planets, comets, galaxies, and space.

caracara A large, long-legged bird of prey living in North and South America.

carambola A yellow tropical fruit which has a star-shaped cross-section when cut through (also known as the star fruit).

cassava A tropical plant with thick roots that are used to make flour and starch.

community A group of people who live in the same neighborhood, such as a village, town, or city.

constellation A group of stars that forms a particular shape in the night sky.

folklore Traditional customs, beliefs, or stories.

piñata A piñata is a clay pot filled with treats. You hang it from a high place then take turns, blindfolded, hitting it with a stick until you get the treats.

pinha Also known as a sugar-apple, this South-American fruit looks a bit like a big pine cone and tastes like custard!

pulses Beans, peas, and lentils – pulses are a cheap, low-fat source of protein.

relief map A map that uses different colors or textures to show high and low ground.

rural Relating to the countryside rather than the town.

Southern Hemisphere The half of the Earth that lies south of the equator.

spoonbill A type of wading bird, with a bill that is rounded and flattened at the tip.

subsidize To help pay for the costs of something.

Further Information

Websites

www.brazilintheschool.org
   Free educational resources for teachers and students, produced by teachers and staff at the Embassy of Brazil.

www.brazil.org.uk/brazilintheschool/brazilforkids.html
   A downloadable, colorful fact sheet takes you on a journey of discovery through rainforests, waterfalls, cities, and beaches.

www.brazilmycountry.com
   Information, city and travel guides; facts on culture, climate, and history.

www.kidscornerbrazil.org
   Information, facts, maps, and games.

kids.nationalgeographic.com/explore/countries/brazil.html
   Facts, geography, nature, people and culture, government, economy, and history.

Further Reading

Barber, Nicola. *Changing World: Brazil*. London, England: Franklin Watts, 2010.

Bingham, Jane. *My Holiday in: Brazil*. London, England: Wayland, 2014.

Morrison, Marion. *Country Files: Brazil*. London, England: Franklin Watts, 2003.

Parker, Edward. *Countries in Our World: Brazil*. London, England: Franklin Watts, 2014.

Savery, Annabel. *My Country: Brazil*. London, England: Franklin Watts, 2014.

Index